C000155933

Structures

poems by

Barry Vitcov

Finishing Line Press
Georgetown, Kentucky

Structures

ACKNOWLEDGMENTS

Every Day We Walk the Same Dusty Path: *Cobra Lily 8,* November, 2022
Nature's Beauty is all the Glamour: *EAP: The Magazine,* Spring 2022
The Sea Is a Bride: *EAP: The Magazine,* Winter 2023

Publisher: Leah Huete de Maines
Editor: Christen Kincaid
Cover Art: William E. Saltzstein
Author Photo: William E. Saltzstein
Cover Design: Elizabeth Maines McCleavy

Order online: www.finishinglinepress.com
also available on amazon.com

Author inquiries and mail orders:
Finishing Line Press
PO Box 1626
Georgetown, Kentucky 40324
USA

Contents

*Dedicated to all the
Southern Oregon poets
who meet monthly to share their poems
with open hearts and thankful applause.
You are a sustaining energy!*

You Hiked Up a Snowy Mountain

You hiked up a rocky, snowy mountain,
stopping to pause at a tall cairn-like shape.
Water flowing like a welcome fountain
over green mossy rocks, an opaque drape
of misty memories. A guiding light
bent by thin air and a tender sweet scent,
while gently remaining out of my sight
as your love was always silently meant.
Climbing higher towards the nearby crest,
slipping slightly on the treacherous trail
seeking freedom in nature's peaceful rest
knowing passion is never for the frail.
You arrive early at a barren butte,
having found a lovely flirtatious route.

Every Day We Walk the Same Dusty Path

Every day we walk the same dusty path
seeking a sense of orderly routine
avoiding an ugly world's toxic wrath
knowing that much beauty is left unseen.
Like the cottonwood waiting for spring leaves
standing bare on a sunny winter's day,
we see a landscape that often deceives
with emptiness and a view of decay.
Yet dreams blossom when we trod this old trail.
Our deciduous nature not asleep,
and our imagination will not fail
to paint a brighter future we can keep.
Chaos is a journey of reflection
sometimes filled with glimpses of perfection.

Ode to Gracie

Her elegance brought beauty to the world
so rarely seen in ordinary dogs.
Casting an aura that captured and furled
through practiced and imagined dialogues.

Doors opened and a leather leash chosen,
she perked knowing it was time for a walk
alert and wagging and poking her nose
to the sidewalk decorated with chalk.
Gracie, the standard poodle, touched my heart
unconditionally when we first met
with boundless joy and cuddles from the start.
And now she has left this earthly home, yet
if angels truly had feathery wings,
she'd be in flight as an angel who sings.

Our Ukraine

We looked to each other with sullen eyes
after the attachment came to a halt
and independence after we cut ties.
You never stopped blaming or finding fault.

Sometimes it's hard to know if family
is family or just an illusion.
It takes distance to understand and see
whether or not real or a delusion.

When, again, we stare with anger and rage,
coming to deadly blows and mortal ends,
will we ever be able to turn a sad page
to a peaceful state and not condescend?

If serenity is merely a dream,
then dreams must be merely a lifelong theme.

Sunday Musing

Be alone with quiet thoughts listening
to the emptiness filled with slow heartbeats.
See the eagerness of hummingbird wings
outside your window. One of nature's feats.
Feel the wind carrying you into flight;
gravity now a foregone illusion,
imagination lifted to new heights
taking you to a wistful conclusion.
A thought interrupted by a poodle
who approaches like a wandering waif
waking you from your dream like a bugle
The reality of the moment safe.
Our minds often escape into a fog
then to be rescued by a loyal dog.

If Music Be

A cacophony of discordant sounds
bouncing helter-skelter about the house
threatening our senses like untamed hounds,
just a musical game of cat and mouse.
If music be the source of lasting love
then surely this noise must be harmonized
before we can look to the sky above
and see melodies played before our eyes.
A concertmaster beginning to tune,
bringing strings, woodwinds, brass, and tympani
from chaos into an orderly room.
The maestro uses his baton to lead
an orchestra filled with a rising tone
that builds to a crescendo fully grown.

Some Thoughts About Thomas Hardy

I thought I heard a knocking at my door
akin to Hardy's digging on his grave.
It happened at my apartment's ground floor.
I saw a dog being walked and I waved.
Hardy wondered what was going on above.
Who was digging and for what good purpose.
He felt the possibility of love
stopping at his final resting surface,
not unlike my thoughts toward that dog walker
with a frisky pup pulling at its leash.
Should I follow and be thought a stalker,
or remain behind closed doors beyond reach?
Questions of love are often confusing.
Hardy's poem helped to make it amusing.

One Night

You turned your back in a splash of color
without so much as a lingering gaze,
which left me alone and feeling smaller,
not part of your impressionable phase.

Our words and touch were filled with tenderness,
the magic only lovers know and trust.
But that bond turned from passion to distress.
Turns out false love was only misplaced lust.

These are the lessons learned from one-night stands:
Don't confuse whispered secrets for allure.
Beauty is more than the caress of hands;
it's something that your spirit must endure.

Go into a dark night with newfound hope
as lovers learn new ways to love and cope.

Old Friends

How do we measure enduring friendship?
Is it the casualness of kindness?
Or the ultimate passion of courtship?
Perhaps a dose of forgiving blindness?

So many years have passed since we first met.
Remembrances of weddings and first born,
rituals enjoyed seem so distant yet
the proverbial wink of an eye warns
of the limitations that time affords
and the need to keep relationships close.
Those gentle embraces and smiles reward
all that we cherish and value the most.

Old friends grow and age as their love endures
the constancy and comfort that matures.

For an Acquaintance and His Wife with Alzheimer's

Who are you to say I would not be there?
After all these years, you still have some doubt
that in the end, when the world seems unfair,
you would be abandoned and left without
someone knowing well your questions and fears.
Although we've often talked of the unknown,
with worry in our hearts and eyes with tears,
we still don't understand being alone
when being together was what we had planned.
Then we were taken to a darker place
where science and reason could not command
answers to what we were forced to embrace.
Knowing faith is as tangible as hope
keeps alive our loving bonds as we cope.

Sitting and Watching

Sitting on a creek-side boulder just after daybreak. Light filtering through dewy air like sprinkles on a donut. It's cool, crisp, and green as he watches for a pair of river otters seen the day before when the fog would not retreat. He is being still, shoulders relaxed, a non-aggressive posture allowing the stream to flow undisturbed. Suddenly slight movements and two otters flip and turn like inverted yo-yos. He tenses with delight.

While behind a tree
blending in with subtlety
among cottonwoods
a crouching force of nature
the cougar waits patiently

DQ Has Opened

Spring continues its zigzag weather pattern, from hot
to cold; sun to rain; maybe a snowflake or two. Winter
was largely a disappointment with its false promise and
ongoing emptiness. Yet not far from my home, a vision. An
unparalleled vision. A love affair from a distance, watching
a beauty arrive like Venus emerging from the sea, lifted on a
scallop shell of questionable repute, born fully grown in her
pink nakedness and flowing hair with Zephyr holding Aura,
both blowing their breezes. I saw the Botticelli at the Uffizi
while being nudged along by impolite travelers, like being in
a school of Branzini. It was a warm day outside and my mind
was focused on gelato, preferably limone and nocciola. But
now, my thoughts wander because it's been months waiting
for another almost mythological event to finally come to
fruition in my hometown. Rising from the ashes of a Burger
King, Dairy Queen takes shape. The Queen has risen in all
her red and white glory, offering an American treat rivaling
Italian memories. Let's chant together, "We all deserve soft
serve! We all deserve soft serve!"

Happiest of days,
I'm ecstatic to report
D.Q. has opened

Lunar Eclipse

We drove up the hill to watch the lunar eclipse, a total eclipse
that had the whole town excited even though the skies were clear
and all we really wanted was more rain. In fact, we wanted all the
rain we could get to break this goddamn drought and feed the
vineyards and orchards, but not the ones run by the cartels who
threaten the peace and steal our water. Yet, we drove up the hill
hoping to get a good view of the eclipse with the poodle in the
back seat and all I could think of was that goddamn Bonnie Tyler
song stuck in my head, "Total Eclipse of the Heart." 'Once upon
a time there was light in my life/But now there's only love in the
dark/Nothing I can say/A total eclipse of the heart.' And there
we were, my wife and the white poodle in the back seat whining
and barking when we got out of the car to watch the total eclipse
of someone else's heart, whose love was apparently in the dark
while there was light in my life. The poodle with the big, fluffy tail
didn't have the same lyric stuck in her head and she didn't even
notice the lunar eclipse, which glowed like a light in the dark, a
total eclipse of the universal heart. And there we were, standing
beside our car in the cool spring air quietly watching the moon's
umbra beginning to glow. I doubt there were Ukrainians mulling
about peering at the lights in their lives.

A light in my life
total eclipse of my heart
just love in the dark

A One-sentence Haibun

There's really very little to fear, unless you consider: rabies; tetanus; alopecia; Mormons at the front door; the doctrine of mutually assured destruction; standing in front of the refrigerator in your underwear holding a head of iceberg lettuce found in the clothes hamper and wondering why there are dirty socks in the vegetable crisper; a four-piece classical chamber ensemble playing interpretations of Billy Joel songs; memories of your mother threatening "wait till your father gets home;" kissing a girl for the first time after just getting braces; coed sex education classes; being the only Jew in your junior high English class and assigned to read the part of Shylock in "The Merchant of Venice"; the Grim Reaper; ingrown toenails; uncontrollable hiccups in the middle of a job interview; and FDR repeating simultaneously like tinnitus in both ears "There is nothing to fear but fear itself."

Whoever said life
is not fair and lighten up
deserves to despair

Thunderstorms Arrive

Thunderstorms arrived
    diving through the valley
with white light shows
    and kettle drumming
booming across the hills
    like a sneering bully with a whip
while Gracie the Poodle
    huddled against my thigh
trembling with fear
    as I soothed her with
caresses and a low, calm voice
    knowing more were on the way:
    another force to bear.

Up All Night

There's nothing to be done
about the staccato drum
of incessant dripping from
some water spilling
      over a clogged
            rain gutter
                  keeping us up all night:

a long run-on sentence of
white noise with exclamation marks.

Seasonal Tanka

Nature's vibrations
awaken all four seasons
like an alarm clock
with automatic settings
of wind, rain, snow and colors.

When I Saw a Love I Would Not Meet

When I saw a love I would not meet
Hesitant to approach or even speak
I stood motionless across the street

Trying to be nonchalant and discreet
She possessed an air and look so unique
When I saw a love I would not meet

If only I had words that might entreat
But I was without courage and weak
I stood motionless across the street

It's one of those times found bittersweet
Like unfulfilled games of hide and seek
When I saw a love I would not meet

It would have been easier to turn and retreat
Instead I remained shyly quiet and meek
I stood motionless across the street

Sometimes life feels incomplete
At turns filled with an odd mystique
When I saw a love I would not meet
I stood motionless across the street

We See the Distant Mountains Snowy Crown

We see the distant mountains snowy crown
melting like a disgraced beauty queen
dashing the hopes of those who have found

the end of a drought from frozen ground.
Wishes often imagine a flirtatious dream
we saw in the distant mountains snowy crown

hoping the earth will be safe and sound,
but, knowing appearance is not what it seems,
dashing the hopes of those who have found

a wish of rain and snow pouring down,
and tempted by the whiteness of the scene
we see in the distant mountains snowy crown.

She was once adored in a flowing white gown
before the shame of it all was clearly seen,
dashing the hopes of those who have found

her to be nothing more than a crazy clown
making our desire for her like a Munchian scream.
When we see the distant mountains snowy crown
dashing the hopes of those who were found.

My Poodle Likes to Chase Her Tail

My poodle likes to chase her tail.
The red cat thinks she's just crazy,
but Emmy goes on without fail.
My poodle likes to chase her tail.
It makes her fitter and more hail,
while the cat stays fat and lazy.
My poodle likes to chase her tail.
The red cat thinks she's just crazy.

It Took Many Years to Lose Her

It took many years to lose her
and an hour to find her again,
fearful some issues might recur.
It took many years to lose her
before longing began to stir.
There are fewer ways to begin.
It took many years to lose her
and an hour to find her again.

Entering Rooms Like a Cipher

Entering rooms like a cipher
nondescript and without pretense
so alone as if a life were
entering rooms like a cipher
surveying all that is right for
just finding a world that makes sense
entering rooms like a cipher
nondescript and without pretense

The Sea Rested from Its Frown

The sea rested from its frown
while we waited for the sun to set...
the sky wearing an orange and red crown.
The sea rested from its frown:
gulls and pelicans a lively sound,
our hands clasped, a calm mood set.
The sea rested from its frown
while we waited for the sun to set.

Nature's Beauty Is All the Glamour

Nature's beauty is all the glamour
one needs on a daily walk,
which my poodle notices in her usual manner.
Nature's beauty is all the glamour,
regardless of how my pup creates a clamor
with all her frolicking and doggy talk.
Nature's beauty is all the glamour
one needs on a daily walk.

The Sea Is a Bride

I found the sea waiting for me,
an old lover calling from the tide
with the rhythmic roar of tympani.
I found the sea waiting for me,
the roll upon roll of the heavy sea
lifting spirits like a waiting bride.
I found the sea waiting for me,
an old lover calling from the tide.

The Plural of Haiku

The plural of haiku is just haiku
It's not really very transformative
Unlike goose to geese not a plural coup
The plural of haiku is just haiku
Sometimes language doesn't have simple clues
Or changes that appear insensitive
The plural of haiku is just haiku
It's not really very transformative

Slate gray skies loom large
hummingbirds flutter below
know about weightless

Tree's feathering arms
seeking upward solitude
remembers its roots

Cottonwood leafing
like an ogre's leering lip
river otters twitch

Smooth river boulders
sentinels in white water
shivering shoulders

Worms slither away
morels appear suddenly
alien lifeforms

Halfway submerged branch
three stones three common mallards
three-year-old delights

Lone hanging branch eyes
spawning Chinook surfacing
splashes of silver

Walk on a fall day
what does the sky surrender
wishes among clouds

Howling winds reveal
contemplative silences
for those who listen

Tulip trees stretching
opening their bells skyward
catching thunderstorms

Single red flower
mingles among waving weeds
bees enjoy the calm

Crater Lake shimmers
blue hues delight a fresh sky
red fox bears witness

Pacific wind blown
poppies sown among purple
thistles glowing bold

Summer lingering
squirrels packing their bounty
pears whisper hello

Mt. Ashland looming
like a ponderous old friend
waiting for new clothes

That dumb woodpecker
again at the chimney flue
Sisyphus risen

Purple hyacinths
blooming among peonies
surprisingly languid

Golden memories
fixing trivia in time
my dog rolls over

Blistered birch branch
beaten beyond tree-like shape
forest listening

Shade-loving Hosta
shelters shadows and green frogs
sunny days beckon

Dogwoods do not bark
cattails purr at river's edge
nature's silent touch

Agates resting here
surrounded by pleasant moss
crawling with black ants

Haiku writers stare
contemplating teacup's leaves
futures seem brighter

Blue sky arranges
trees among green acres and
branches frame my thoughts

Single spike of grass
growing slender in the dune
ocean waves edge closer

Seagull pivots left
then turns right into the fog
ocean buoy clangs

Long-billed shorebird pokes
hundreds of holes in the sand
tiny fleas disperse

A star shines within
many moons illuminate
an ocean captures

Fronds feather upward
bushes silently creaking
happy birds singing

Lightning strikes abound
round and round the valley's hills
silent sounds scattered

A flutter of winds
blackbirds rushing among leaves
delights Raywood Ash

Hear a whoosh of wings
a cluster of whispering
Whip-poor-wills singing

Dragonfly hovers
within a pond's border reeds
darts off and returns

Cardinals surround
a pleasant juniper bush
before flying off

Where a broken branch
angles slowly from its trunk
new green leaves unfold

Summer's gentle breeze
moves wavelike through the window
my warm arm is cooled

Humidity hangs
softly in red flamed maples
butterflies skirt by

Blackbird stares sideways
vigilant in its darting
quick chirp bids farewell

Marguerite daisies
open to the sun and heat
petals torn by wind

Summer becomes fall
Canadian maples bloom
tangerine and cool

Waves move like popcorn
three-quarter moon softens sky
walkers notice birds

Dandelions grow
where the grass tends to lie low
white tops seek the sun

Fresh orange pumpkins
tacitly absorb sunlight
rotting to its core

Unbroken blue sky
lays atop rolling green hills
the horizon sleeps

Mother-In-Law's tongue
wagging viperlike poems
beckoning no one

Barry Vitcov is a retired educator having spent 45 years as a middle school English teacher, school administrator, leadership coach, and adjunct university professor. He lives in Ashland, Oregon with his wife and exceptionally brilliant standard poodle. As a teenager, he fondly remembers his father carrying a small collection of his poems in his billfold and showing them off to friends and customers. Barry was raised in the San Francisco Bay Area where he was privileged to experience the 1960's energy, diversity and music as a high school and college student. While attending San Fernando Valley State College (now California State University, Northridge), he was mentored by Newdigate Prize winning poet David Posner, professor and poet Benjamin Saltman and creative writing professor Wallace Graves. The lessons from those three extraordinary teachers have served as a lifelong influence on Barry's poetry and narrative writing. During his educational career, he wrote very little fiction and poetry, as he was immersed in his work. After retirement, he began writing again and continues to hone his literary voice. He has had fiction and poetry published in *EAP: The Magazine, Literary Yard, Scarlet Leaf Review, Vita Brevis, Finding the Birds, Cobra Lily,* and *The Drabble*. Finishing Line Press published two of his books, a poetry collection *Where I Live Some of the Time* (2021) and a collection of short stories *The Wilbur Stories & More* (2022). FLP will publish a novella *The Boy with Six Fingers* in June 2025.

Milton Keynes UK
Ingram Content Group UK Ltd.
UKHW012002020524
442050UK00004B/225